The Mockingbird

NUMBER ELEVEN
THE CORRIE HERRING HOOKS SERIES

ROBIN W. DOUGHTY

The Mockingbird

UNIVERSITY OF TEXAS PRESS
AUSTIN

First edition, 1988

Requests for permission to reproduce material
from this work should be sent to
Permissions, University of Texas Press,
Box 7819, Austin, Texas 78713-7819.

LIBRARY OF CONGRESS
CATALOGING-IN-PUBLICATION DATA

Doughty, Robin W.
    The Mockingbird / Robin W. Doughty.—
    1st ed.   p.   cm.—(The Corrie Herring
    Hooks series ; no. 11)
    Bibliography: p.
    ISBN 0-292-75099-4
    1. Mockingbirds.   I. Title.   II. Series:
Corrie Herring Hooks series ; 11.
    QL696.P25D68   1988
    598.8'41—dc19   88-736
                                         CIP

Contents

STEVEN HOLT / VIREO

Acknowledgments

I am extremely grateful to a number of people who have offered comments, suggestions, and information about mockingbirds. Cheryl A. Logan read the manuscript and provided expert help in interpreting song and territorial behavior. Robert Hudson and Michael J. Rogers sent me information about errant mockingbirds in the United Kingdom. I thank staff members, especially Linda Birch, at the Alexander Library, Edward Grey Institute of Field Ornithology, Oxford, for access to sources for the Mimidae. Alfonso Ortiz suggested sources for Hispanic and Pueblo Indian accounts of the mockingbird. Alan Friedman drew my attention to the treatment of the mockingbird in American poetry and prose and commented helpfully about interpretation. Barbara Parmenter carefully perused all aspects of the project. I am most indebted to her.

I also am most appreciative to the University of Texas Research Institute for a grant to assist with data retrieval and illustrations. John Cotter assisted with the maps, and the staff in the University of Texas Department of Geography, Beverly Beaty-Benadom, Bob Wolfkill, and Gary Wahlen, gave vital clerical assistance. Thank you all.

MOCKBIRD

Trim bird snags   insect
   in   the usual
   way   tugs berry
               then on

    that special
perch combs   feather
        deigns   mimic
a bluejay   glitter

eye from   trapeze
            scuffs
   cat and   inhales
heaven with spread soft

           wings
   shouting   joy in
    every corner
talisman in

    my yard dappled
friend with   kin
  you   build
        a fort

  from edges guard
    the perimeter
in   which our hopes
  survive

          R.W.D.

The Mockingbird

The mockingbird's invention is limitless;
he strews newness about as casually as a god.
—Annie Dillard,
Pilgrim at Tinker Creek

The mockingbird has no color, no peculiarity of form, is of
conventional size for the passerine order to which he belongs,
never appears in great numbers, can't be eaten, and is not a
pest unless there is ripe fruit about the place . . .

Yet inconspicuous as he is in appearance, if a poll were
taken throughout his range, he would come forward in the
upper five per cent of the birds readily recognized. . . . It is
the mockingbird's personality, even more than his song, which
distinguishes him. He has qualities we admire and talk about.
—Roy Bedichek,
Adventures with a Texas Naturalist

Introduction

*M*ay Day's early evening haze—sign of summer breath-to-be—carries a mockingbird chorale over Austin, Texas. The male has chosen to sing again from the topmost branch of a mulberry tree. He shouts both day and night from his special perch in the city heart. Below him, three well-grown youngsters squeak hoarsely, begging for food. Sometimes the mocker will carry them a beetle or moth. At other times he will bring a mulberry or peck deeply into a nearby loquat, yellowed to sweet plumpness. Without a prolonged spell of cold weather these plants have flourished and are loaded with glowing fruit. Neighborhood squirrels, which the mocker chases fiercely, feast on them, too.

The parents have delivered the young safely. Their progeny left the nest six days ago and already demonstrate typical poise and alertness. They are beginning to look like the adults except for stubby tails and the need to balance more expertly on breeze-driven limbs. The young birds teeter ominously on such exposed branches, but so far cats have failed to pounce on an individual fluttering on the ground.

High above, dark swifts paint the blue sky in feather parabolas. They have been here a month and have sorted out squabbles over chimney nest sites. At the end of the block Cedar Waxwings, out of range of the mockingbird, are gobbling loquats. They have been around longer, for much of the winter, and are heading north. By the time they mate and nest, the mockingbird pair may well be into its third brood. Then, it will be hot in central Texas. Now, spring shows off new things. The neighborhood is brimful of the mocker's chant. Life is fulfilled. He is the spirit of ebullience in us all—a symbol of renewal.

Such dramas occur repeatedly throughout the mockingbird's range. America's so-called national songbird floods much of the country's springtime with joyful sound. Its song demands our attention. We enjoy its companionship. We admire the resourcefulness and determination by which parent birds drive away cats, jays, and similar intruders from a nesting territory. Such a melodious voice and strong attachments to home mark out this bird. Poets, novelists, and nature writers celebrate its spirit of indomitability, casting the mockingbird as the embodiment of the South, the bird's stronghold, where warm, scented airs quaver to the tumult of the "King of Song." They admire the bird's practice of singing at night and its ability to imitate other species. What the mockingbird lacks in color, it gains in shape, poise, sound, and interesting habits.

This book examines these fascinating characteristics. It discusses the Northern Mockingbird's life history and distribution, and how, unlike so many other species, in recent decades this bird has pioneered new range in North America. The mockingbird prospers biologically and captures our hearts. By declaring it the official state bird of five states, Americans have demonstrated just how special this songbird is, spinning myths about its boldness, intelligence, and vocal dexterity. This book details the strength of our very special bond with an animal that adds zest to our lives.

The Mockingbirds

*T*he term "mockingbird" applies to fourteen of the thirty-two or so species of the Mimidae family of "Mimic-Thrushes," named after their abilities to imitate the sounds of other birds. The Northern Mockingbird, *Mimus polyglottos,* belongs to the ten-member genus *Mimus* within this family. *Mimus* is Latin for "mimic," and is derived from the Greek word *mimos,* or "imitator." This polyglot, or "many-tongued mimic," is the northernmost and one of the most widespread and best known of all mockingbirds.

Avian systematists have usually placed the mockingbird close to the wrens and thrushes. New biochemical studies using a DNA hybridization technique reveal that mockingbirds and thrashers are more closely related to Old World starlings than to any other living taxon. Yale University researchers Charles G. Sibley and Jon E. Ahlquist conclude that the Mimidae family, which also includes the well-known Gray Catbird and Brown Thrasher, may have evolved from a common starling-type ancestor twenty-three to twenty-eight million years ago.

All mimid species are found in the Americas, ranging from southern Canada to Argentina and Chile. Ten species, including *Mimus polyglottos,* live mostly north of Mexico. At the other end of the New World, the Patagonian Mockingbird (*M. patagonicus*) inhabits the open, exposed south lands of Tierra del Fuego. Two or three other mockingbirds have made their home in the balmier climes of Caribbean islands. One of these, the Bahama Mockingbird (*M. gundlachii*), has turned up on the Florida Keys.

Another mockingbird, *Neosomimus trifasciatus,* is restricted to the Galapagos Islands. Ornithologists debate whether the three or four mockers on different places in that archipelago are races or separate species of the Galapagos Mockingbird; or, in fact, whether they are closely related to the Long-tailed Mockingbird (*M. longicaudatus*) of the South American mainland, and therefore, should be included in the genus *Mimus.* Of historical interest is the work by Frank J. Sulloway indicating

[13]

that it was the Galapagos Mockingbirds, not Galapagos finches, that were important in Charles Darwin's thinking about the theory of evolution.

The "Mimic-Thrushes" are noted for their long tails and rounded or fairly short wings, which enable them to pivot and maneuver in dense foliage close to the ground. Some of them, particularly thrashers, tend to run more than fly and give the impression of being rather shy. Most merge with the background because they are nondescript in color, tending to gray, brown, or gray-brown. Some have streaked or spotted breasts with white patches on the wings or tail; and all of them possess relatively long, downcurved bills with which they forage in the leaf litter after insects, seeds, and berries.

The Northern Mockingbird, similar in size to the American Robin, shows pale gray to white underparts and buffy gray to gray upperparts with white wing patches that flash conspicuously in flight. Its long, slender tail sports white outer feathers. Superficially, the mocker resembles the slightly smaller Loggerhead Shrike, which has a black facial mask. The shrike, however, flies with fast wingbeats in a more direct, less undulating manner than the mockingbird, and shows less white on the wings.

What the mockingbird family lacks in coloration is certainly made up for by the strong, varied song of many members. The Northern Mockingbird, in particular, is one of the most appreciated of all American songbirds. Living up to its Latin name, it imitates the calls and songs of other birds with remarkable precision. The versatility, consistency, and volume of its voice capture our attention. Its boldness and a confiding nature around people, evidenced by a liking for gardens, parks, and suburban areas, increase our admiration and respect.

The famous Swedish taxonomist Karl von Linné (Linnaeus), founder of the binomial system of plant and animal classification, named the Northern Mockingbird *Turdus polyglottos*, placing it among the thrushes from information supplied to him by an English gentleman of leisure, Mark Catesby (1683–1749). Lauded by historian Elsa G. Allen as the "first real naturalist in America," Catesby made two visits to the American colonies between 1712 and 1726 from which he compiled a two-volume *Natural History of Carolina, Florida and the Bahama Islands* (1731), consisting of 220 plates of 109 bird species. By the time of Catesby's visits, the initial awe felt by Europeans confronted with the plethora of New World plants and animals had given way to curiosity and resource-minded pragmatism. Such realism is reflected in Catesby's accurate illustrations of New World plants and animals.

In his first volume, the naturalist furnished more than 100 plates of North American birds, one of which (Plate 27) showed "The Mock-Bird, *Turdus minor cinereo albus non maculatus*," or the gray-white, non-streaked small thrush, posed alertly on a branch of flowering dogwood. Although Mark Catesby provided details about fewer than 25 percent of eastern U.S. bird species, the ones he did note, such as the "mock-bird," were precise and of high quality. Linnaeus was indebted to Catesby, who naturally applied many of the common names of English birds to species in America that resembled them, as with the superficial resemblance of the mockingbird to a thrush.

MOCKINGBIRDS IN THE GENUS *Mimus*	
Species	*Common Name*
M. polyglottos	Northern Mockingbird
M. gilvus[a]	Tropical Mockingbird
M. magnirostris[b]	St. Andrew Mockingbird
M. gundlachii	Bahama Mockingbird
M. thenca	Chilean Mockingbird
M. longicaudatus	Long-tailed Mockingbird
M. saturninus	Chalk-browed Mockingbird
M. patagonicus	Patagonian Mockingbird
M. triurus	White-banded Mockingbird
M. dorsalis	Brown-backed Mockingbird

[a] Some authors combine it with *M. polyglottos.*
[b] Possible race of *M. gilvus.*

LAURA RILEY

Distribution

The Mimidae family's range encompasses more than one hundred degrees of latitude in North and South America. The Northern Mockingbird occurs in approximately one-third of this band and is spread across an even larger longitudinal zone spanning more than three thousand miles in North America. Within this area the mockingbird is separated into a western race and an eastern race. The slightly larger, paler western race, *Mimus polyglottos leucopterus,* occurs from northern California across most of Nevada, Utah, southeast Wyoming into southwest South Dakota, and south throughout much of the western United States into Baja California and southern Mexico (Oaxaca and Vera Cruz), where it occasionally breeds with the Tropical Mockingbird, *M. gilvus.* Hybrids have been collected on the Isthmus of Tehuantepec, leading some to discuss whether the Tropical Mockingbird is a race of *M. polyglottos.*

The eastern race, *M. p. polyglottos,* a smaller, darker bird, replaces the western form in east central Texas and Oklahoma and is a resident throughout the South. It inhabits the Florida Keys, the Greater Antilles (including Little Cayman east to the Virgin Islands), and the Bahama Islands, where its range overlaps with that of the Bahama species, *M. gundlachii.* Both mockingbird species inhabit semi-dense scrub, but the northern mocker is more numerous near human habitations, preferring the edges of clearings as in the United States. There are records of interbreeding.

The eastern race of the mockingbird breeds regularly as far north as New York State and New England; it spreads across Pennsylvania, Ohio, Indiana, and central Illinois into southern Iowa. It merges with the western race in Nebraska and Kansas.

The mockingbird is much more localized along the northern edge of its range, which it is expanding. The South, however, remains its true home. It is especially abundant in Texas. Federally sponsored Breeding Bird Surveys, conducted annually in late May and early June, consistently pick up high numbers on the Rio Grande Plain and the eastern edge of the Edwards Plateau. Each census route covers twenty-five miles and consists of fifty stopping points.

Sixteen of the 140 census routes in Texas average a high for the nation of one hundred or more mockingbirds, and two of them, in the Rio Grande Valley's 2.2-million-acre Webb County, hold at least two hundred birds each. Speaking about

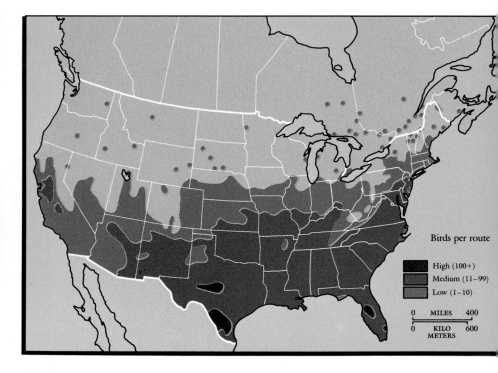

Relative abundance of the Northern Mockingbird in the United States and Canada.

Map by J. V. Cotter, after Chandler S. Robbins et al., *The Breeding Bird Survey: Its First Fifteen years, 1965–1979* (U.S. Fish and Wildlife Service, Resource Publication 57, 1986).

the mesquite-and-cactus-filled brushlands between Hebbron-ville and the Rio Grande, nature writer Roy Bedichek believed that "This kind of country in the Southwest supports more mockingbirds per acre than any other." Bird survey statistics confirm his belief that the mockers "tyrannize over other bird life by weight of numbers as well as by individual prowess."

Another center of abundance in Texas is in the "Hill Country" along the eastern edge of the Edwards Plateau, the rolling, predominantly limestone upland terminus of North America's Great Plains. About half-a-dozen census routes there consistently turn up 100 or more mockers. One of them, in Llano County, shows about 150 individuals, with several birds found regularly at almost every one of the stopping places. Mockingbirds seem to take charge and stake a claim to this land worn down by decades of overgrazing. As dawn breaks, their voices swell up to dominate softer notes made by Northern Cardinals, Eastern Phoebes, and Painted Buntings. They flash down like shrikes to pounce on a bug on the ground or one suspended in the blanket of wildflowers. Often the male will float aloft on spread wings from the tip of a high post oak, leaping up and floating down as he gushes sound. Birds chase one another, corkscrewing among mesquite, climbing in and out of mistletoe clumps, disputing constantly about fiefdoms and boundaries. Some adults escort hoarse-sounding young, grabbing up insects for them, warding off strangers as they nurture a new generation. Others are sentinels checking for dangers.

In the Texas Hill Country, mockingbird song and mimicry dominate spring. At times the bird's renditions of the Northern Bobwhite whistle, Cactus Wren churr, or Scissor-tailed Flycatcher squawk make its voice difficult to separate from those of the true callers. But often the male mocker gives himself away by returning too quickly to the imitation or repeating it too many times. Mockingbirds live in this open oak-and-mesquite-dotted grassland all year, but they are most noticeable in late May and early June, when their activities and voices fill up the open landscape, making it shimmer to the sound and bustle of their lives.

Range Extension

*I*ts preference for humanly modified and cleared habitats helps explain the extension of the Northern Mockingbird's range. Mockingbirds frequent subdivisions, schoolyards, and recreational areas in which native plants mixed with introduced ornamentals provide edible fruits and berries. The birds readily adapt to human presence and sing from housetops, utility poles, transmission wires, and roadside fences. Mockingbirds will also visit bird feeders when raisins, grapes, and other suitable foods, plus water sources, are set out. Our habit of augmenting natural foods with handouts assists this and many other species, especially seed-eating birds. Experts believe that this is another factor in the mockingbird's gradual northward push over the past half-century or so. The sleek gray bird remains unusual as a resident in many northern states, but numbers are growing, although nesting data from the entire country show a slight decline from the mid-1960s through the 1970s.

Between 1900 and 1920, ornithologist Horace W. Wright reported that the Northern Mockingbird was very rare in New England. Since Wright's time, the number of sightings has increased markedly, so that today, on Long Island, for instance, where as a boy Theodore Roosevelt mentioned the mockingbird as rare, the species is quite common. Stragglers on Long Island and elsewhere have faced a number of difficulties. Wright reported that collectors, including ornithologists eager for specimens, shot mockingbirds. Winter weather also killed off all but the hardiest individuals by cutting off supplies of insects and berries. Bird lovers began to show generosity toward a few mockingbirds that showed up around houses. They set out crumbs, meat, fruit, and other tidbits, enabling at least a few to survive. Clearly then, even before the craze for backyard feeders gained its strongest momentum, well-intentioned people took an active, sustained interest in birdlife around their homes.

New York State exemplifies best the bird's push northward. The first authenticated nesting occurred in 1925 (in Erie

County), and in the past thirty years or so more than one hundred records of breeding are recorded. As in New England, the Northern Mockingbird began pushing slowly into the upper Midwest in the nineteenth century. Sporadic occurrences, even breeding, showed up ahead of occupation of suitable habitat. During the 1880s, a few mockingbirds nested in north Macoupin County and Livingston County in central Illinois a good fifty years before a major surge took place in the state's southern counties. The same unusual distribution existed in nearby Michigan, where the mockingbird was first listed in 1839, becoming a rare summer resident mostly in the lower peninsula's southern half, but with single birds popping up as far north as Lake Superior's Isle Royale.

A brake to this overall push northward has been the reduction of woody vegetation around buildings and field boundaries in the farm belt. In central and northern Illinois, for instance, agribusiness with an accent on pesticides and expansion of large fields for mechanized farming has destroyed many of the woody kinds of places and field edges in which mockingbirds and other passerines find food and cover.

The Northern Mockingbird appears regularly as both a summer resident and a winter visitor in Minnesota. Spring migrants move in from mid-April through May, and fall records occur through late November. First listed in 1883 (in Otter Tail County), nesting was not confirmed until 1968 at Royalton, Morrison County, although it was suspected forty-five years earlier. Most wintering birds die off, but some have survived in the Twin Cities area.

Further north, in Canada, Horace Wright enumerated five occurrences of northern mockers, dating back to June 1860, when a single mockingbird was killed as it perched on a barn in Chatham, Ontario. Two birds turned up in Ontario in the 1880s, and two more appeared in Nova Scotia, one of which, a juvenile, was on Sable Island. Another mocker followed it there in September 1902. Wright concluded in 1921 that except for the western end of Lake Erie, where the Northern Mockingbird appeared to be establishing a foothold, the species was rare in Canada. Since then, however, the gray bird has become

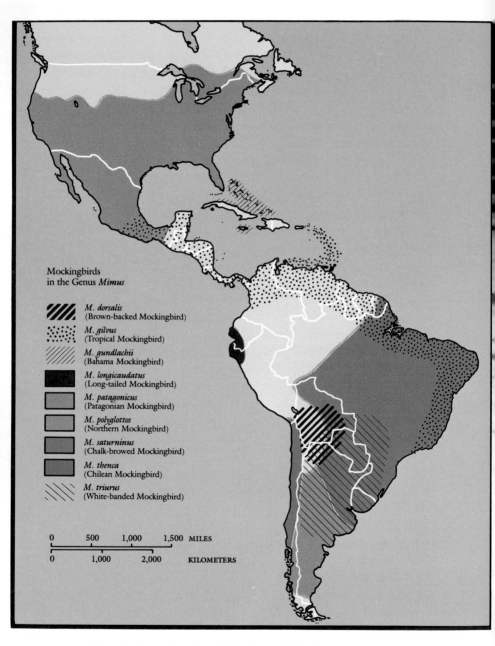

Mockingbirds
in the Genus *Mimus*

M. dorsalis
(Brown-backed Mockingbird)

M. gilvus
(Tropical Mockingbird)

M. gundlachii
(Bahama Mockingbird)

M. longicaudatus
(Long-tailed Mockingbird)

M. patagonicus
(Patagonian Mockingbird)

M. polyglottos
(Northern Mockingbird)

M. saturninus
(Chalk-browed Mockingbird)

M. thenca
(Chilean Mockingbird)

M. triurus
(White-banded Mockingbird)

| 0 | 500 | 1,000 | 1,500 MILES |

| 0 | 1,000 | 2,000 | KILOMETERS |

Distribution of mockingbirds (genus *Mimus*).
Map by J. V. Cotter

a localized resident in eastern Canada, slowly spreading north-ward over the course of the last forty or fifty years. The North-ern Mockingbird remains rare in British Columbia, and occurs locally and irregularly in Edmonton, Calgary, and a few other locations in Alberta, usually in spring or fall. A mocker in Calgary fed on berries and survived −24°F temperatures in the winter of 1958−1959 before it disappeared.

In neighboring Saskatchewan, *Mimus polyglottos* has appeared in no fewer than eight localities, including Regina, Saskatoon, and Prince Albert; and in Manitoba, it has appeared as far north as Churchill. People have found nests in Ontario, Quebec, Nova Scotia, and Newfoundland.

Ornithologist Paul A. Johnsgard states that the usual limit of the mockingbird's nesting range in the U.S. plains states is northern Nebraska, although a few birds occur and probably breed in the Dakotas. As far back as November 1916, a "straggler" turned up on the University of North Dakota campus, and the species is tagged as a "hypothetical" breeder in that state; that is, over the years there are enough scattered records of single birds during summer months to suggest that the species is nesting.

West of the continental divide, this *Mimus* species has a sparser distribution along the same band of latitude. In the early 1970s, Thomas Dearborn Burleigh found only three earlier records for Idaho, but speculated that the mocker may be looked for increasingly in the southern part of that state.

Southward in the basin and range country the mockingbird is more common and widespread. It nests regularly in the semi-arid brushlands of Utah, being most abundant along the lower reaches of the Virgin and Colorado rivers. It is also widely seen in Arizona and New Mexico, where it is a summer resident virtually statewide, from lowlands upward to 8,000 feet above sea level. The mockingbird shares space with five other family members, namely the Gray Catbird and four species of thrasher, though it occupies different habitat in these arid states.

The mockingbird's range expansion northward is shared with other species, notably but not exclusively seed-eating birds. When the food supply expands, some bird populations

[23]

build up rapidly. The number of Red-winged Blackbirds, for example, has soared as new methods of grain harvesting have enabled them to dwell all year in much of the grainbelt. Gull populations have climbed in response to municipal garbage dumps that provide excellent sites for scavenging, particularly in coastal communities. An enormous increase in bird feeders has benefitted the Northern Cardinal, Tufted Titmouse, and House Finch. These birds, like the Northern Mockingbird, have also expanded their ranges northward. The mockingbird has probably benefitted from such human generosity as well as from the regrowth of woody vegetation in fields, the spread of brush, and, of course, legal protection (see "Cage Birds and Conservationists").

The precise mechanisms by which the mocker has gone north while the American Robin and Barn Swallow have spread south as breeders remain unclear. Nonetheless, the fact that these species seem to be expanding when the ranges of so many others appear to be shrinking is heartening. Some of this expansion is due to the introduction of birds to new areas in order to "improve" the existing fauna. Historically, people have welcomed the arrival of the Northern Mockingbird as an improvement on local fauna.

Introductions and Arrivals

*M*ockingbirds, as we shall see, figured prominently in the cage bird traffic during the nineteenth century because of their reputations as fine singers. Other efforts were also underway to import and establish songbirds in the wild. The mockingbird was an obvious candidate, together with more exotic European and Asian thrushes, finches, and, of course, the nightingale. The fad for adding to America's avifauna centered initially in Brooklyn, New York, where at mid-century the House Sparrow, an Old World native, soon to become a pest, received an enthusiastic greeting. Acclimatization Societies grew up in many communities in order to import scores of species which wealthy residents and others with strong European roots desired to have around their homes.

Between 1872 and 1874, the Cincinnati Acclimatization Society set free three thousand birds belonging to about twenty species at an approximate cost of $9,000. In the same decade, the American Acclimatization Society, under the leadership of philanthropist Eugene Schieffelin, liberated foreign birds in New York's Central Park. Schiefflin's purpose was to introduce all the birds mentioned in the works of William Shakespeare. Between 1889 and 1908 the Song Bird Club of Portland, Oregon, founded by a German-American, C. F. Pfluger, made strenuous efforts to introduce European larks, thrushes, and finches as well as American mockingbirds to the West Coast. After a perfunctory attempt to acclimate the captive birds, the survivors were liberated on the outskirts of Portland and elsewhere, but not before "Thousands of people went to see them, and the society realized about five hundred dollars by this show," according to Pfluger, as quoted by Gene Stratton Porter. Further south in the San Francisco Bay area similar attempts also included nightingales and native mockingbirds.

In March 1891, bolstered by favorable reports, the Oregon-based society ordered additional birds at a cost of more than $750. The various species included "twenty-four pairs of American mocking-birds at $5.50 per pair." These were mixed in with an assortment of European larks, thrushes, warblers, robins, and finches.

In a statement, Pfluger claimed that in Oregon the pale, trim mockingbirds prospered—at least initially. Another lot of sixty-seven pairs was purchased and forty pairs received their freedom in 1895; all, however, seem to have dispersed or dwindled rapidly. John C. Phillips reports that a similar fate befell other Northern Mockingbirds released by "the country club at San Francisco with birds ordered from Louisiana in 1891." A competing vocalist, the Old World nightingale, fared just as badly.

CLAY ELLIS

Island Colonization

The mockingbird's vocal abilities are not especially impaired when it is kept in captivity, and this quality, plus its durability and trim appearance, made it a candidate for transport and release beyond the boundaries of the continental United States. Mockingbirds comprised part of the traffic in colorful buntings, insect-sized hummingbirds, and scarlet-tinted cardinals sent overseas to amuse courtesans and wealthy merchants in the eighteenth and nineteenth centuries. North American birds added a distinctly exotic flavor to Europe's better-known aviaries. Some of these distant places across the Pacific and Atlantic oceans also became home territories for the mockingbird. In this way, for example, the mockingbird and a host of other birds and mammals established themselves in Hawaii.

The Northern Mockingbird is now a permanent resident of Hawaii, whose indigenous flora and fauna have undergone immense change. In the late eighteenth century, Europeans introduced cattle, horses, goats, sheep, and other domestic animals, which ravaged the native vegetation. Game mammals followed, and in many cases went wild like other livestock. Some, like the wild goat, continue to thrive in very rugged terrain and overgraze the range, causing erosion. Native birds, already buffeted by logging, agriculture, and settlement, have also had to cope with alien species. In general, the specialized island fauna usually fails to compete with hardier, more adaptable species introduced from the mainland. Since 1796, 170 bird species have been released in Hawaii and many have succeeded in displacing endemic species.

George C. Munro, expert on Hawaiian birds, notes that the Northern Mockingbird is a more recent newcomer, introduced from the U.S. mainland in 1928. It was "established on Oahu and probably elsewhere. I saw it on Maui and I think on Hawaii in 1936." Most authorities attribute the mockingbird's successful colonization to the Hui Manu, a Honolulu-based group whose purpose was to introduce songbirds and insectivorous species to Hawaii. The Hui Manu freed mockingbirds on

Oahu from 1931 to 1933, and on Maui in 1933. Their introductions took hold, and the species is now established throughout the state.

On Mexico's Socorro Island, 250 miles off Baja California, the endemic Socorro Mockingbird (*Mimodes graysoni*), previously called a thrasher, has been diminished to the point of extinction, while the newcomer *Mimus polyglottos* has established itself by flying in from the continental mainland. An immigrant has moved in to supplant an indigenous species. Researchers Joseph R. Jehl and Kenneth C. Parkes, who have followed the buildup of the Northern Mockingbird population on this Mexican island, believe that although human transport was not involved, other human activities directly contributed to the survival of the northern mocker and hastened the demise of the Socorro native. They cite the provision of fresh-water ponds, gardens, and orchards around the island's military base as a boon for any exhausted migrants, and note that open habitats created by sheep grazing offer an "appropriate vacant 'niche'" for the Northern Mockingbird. In addition, they believe that the extraordinary tameness, curiosity, and aboriginal abundance of the Socorro Mockingbird made it vulnerable to cats, which were initially transported to the military base in the 1950s. There were no native mammals on Socorro, and those birds accustomed to foraging on the ground fell easy prey to alien cats.

The Northern Mockingbird has disappeared from Barbados, where it was introduced; it also died out on Bermuda, where the species met with temporary success from 1893 to about 1914. The German consul, Captain Meyer, reportedly liberated six pairs of *M. polyglottos* at St. George's in 1893. All went well for about twenty years, although the mocker never increased as rapidly as people had expected, given the fact that a relative, the Gray Catbird, was abundant. In 1914, however, a visitor remarked that "quite a number" existed on this Atlantic Ocean archipelago. But the mocker was unable to sustain itself some six hundred miles from the U.S. mainland. By the early 1930s "no recent observations" existed, and today the songster no longer inhabits Bermuda, nor St. Helena, even further out in the Atlantic Ocean, where people also released it.

Interestingly, *M. polyglottos* appears to have flown across the Atlantic Ocean to the British Isles on no less than three occasions. Concern about whether these Northern Mockingbirds were "escapes" has postponed recognition of them as bona fide wild birds. The British Ornithologists' Union (B.O.U.) Records Committee accepted identification from a sight record (with photographs) at Worm's Head, West Glamorgan, Wales, from 24 July to 11 August 1978, but rejected this mockingbird as first for the United Kingdom on the grounds that "it was considered probably an escape from captivity in view of the species' sedentary nature in North America."

A recent study by Chandler S. Robbins concerning thirty-eight American bird species likely to be added to an already lengthy list of vagrants in the United Kingdom and Ireland, suggests, however, that the Northern Mockingbird is indeed a passerine to be looked for, notably in autumn. This prediction is founded on three factors. First, the mockingbird is abundant along the Atlantic seaboard of the United States; second, it migrates or disperses in fall months from the northern parts of its range; third, it has the right body size and flight speed necessary to make a nonstop water crossing of at least 1,700 miles. This assessment is making British ornithologists rethink their previous position about the mockingbird being "sedentary" or unlikely to fly far enough to land in Britain.

Two additional instances of mockingbirds in the British Isles remain under review. One record dates back to 22 August 1971, when a Northern Mockingbird was seen on Norfolk's Blakeney Point—an east coast locality famous for rare migrants, usually from Scandinavia or Siberia. The B.O.U.'s committee was unable to secure photographic evidence to substantiate identification. The second bird appeared on the Atlantic coast at Saltash, Cornwall, on 30 August 1982. The Rarities Committee accepted this record and has passed it along to the B.O.U. Records Committee, which has yet to make a pronouncement. It seems quite possible that *M. polyglottos* will join the ranks of other North American species that have made an official landfall in the United Kingdom.

Robin W. Doughty

LEROY WILLIAMSON / TEXAS PARKS & WILD

Life History: Food

The Northern Mockingbird, like its relatives the Gray Catbird and Brown Thrasher, subsists mainly on insects, berries,
and seeds. But unlike the Brown Thrasher, which consumes
about two-thirds animal matter (mostly insects), the mockingbird's diet is slightly more vegetable than animal. Arthur Cleveland Bent, whose 1948 volume on the life history of North
America's birds remains a very useful though dated source,
noted that about 48 percent of mocker foods were beetles, ants,
grasshoppers, spiders, etc., consumed most abundantly during
the May breeding season, while plant materials made up the
remaining 52 percent.

The bird's penchant for fruits and berries of holly, smilax,
woodbine, sumac, and other plants extends to garden and hor-
ticultural crops such as grapes, blackberries, and figs. A habit of
raiding garden patches for these succulent fruits earned the
gray-colored species a dubious reputation. An 1897 list of birds
beneficial to agriculture included hawks, owls, cuckoos, woodpeckers, and the more common garden varieties such as robins,
wrens, and chickadees, but failed to include any American
mimids despite the prodigious numbers of insects they consumed. Bent reported that one grape grower near St. Au-
gustine, Florida, killed 1,100 mockingbirds for daring to invade
his vineyard, and, out of retribution it seems, buried their
bodies beneath the vines. Other growers in the South also
grumbled about the mockingbird's liking for fruit; but around
the turn of the present century, when ornithologists analyzed
items in bird stomachs, they volunteered, albeit timidly, that
there was "nothing to prove that the Mockingbird eats domestic fruit to an injurious extent."

More forthright support came from researchers of crop pests.
William L. McAtee, a federal biologist studying the economic
importance of birds to agriculture, noted that 48 percent of 417
stomachs of Northern Mockingbirds collected in the South
contained animal matter. Significantly, food remains included
harmful weevils, cucumber beetles, chinch bugs, and grass-

hoppers. Domestic fruit, mostly raspberries or blackberries, formed merely 3 percent of stomach contents. McAtee concluded that the mocker's habit of feasting on cotton worms and boll weevils made it, on balance, much more deserving of attention from horticulturalists, including those Floridians and Texans who had objected to losing grapes and figs.

The mockingbird's somewhat drab appearance and its qualified usefulness to agriculture did not recommend it for universal recognition and admiration, and certainly would not have impelled five legislatures to enshrine it as a state bird. Two activities vital to reproduction have given the species unique qualities. First, the Northern Mockingbird establishes and defends a specific area or territory by what in human eyes is bold, daring, and tenacious behavior. Bird lovers have always praised the mockingbird for the care, fidelity, and perseverance it demonstrates in guarding a territory, nest, and young. At the turn of this century when public interest in birds was heightened by popular books and articles, conservationists tended to promote common familiar species virtually as "little people" capable of instructing school children in civic virtues. The "bold" mockingbird suggested how individualism and competition improved one's lot, while the bird's willingness to assert itself for the good of dependents and friends promoted community values.

Second, people from all walks of life derive pleasure and inspiration from the complexity of the mockingbird's song, which combines melody with mimicry in a way that outshines the Brown Thrasher and Gray Catbird, also noted for their fine voices. This loud, ebullient, varied, and prolonged singing, combined with fearlessness and what people regard as affection for human habitations, separates the mockingbird from other species.

Mockingbird bravely attacking
a bald eagle that has invaded its territory.

Territory

Two groups of researchers in the early 1930s unlocked the mysteries of Northern Mockingbird behavior and life history. Amelia Laskey, working with both caged and wild mockingbirds in Nashville, Tennessee, published several important papers about biology and territoriality. Her nationally acclaimed studies drew upon data from more than 250 nests, from over 900 banded nestlings, and from careful observations she made on individual birds.

On the West Coast, Harold and Josephine Michener conducted a careful, remarkably detailed study of mockingbirds around their home a mile from downtown Pasadena, California. Their residential lot measured 100 by 370 feet and included eucalyptus trees and a variety of shrub species in what they called a "feral garden." The Micheners had operated a bird banding station in their garden for eight years prior to 1933, when they decided to add color bands to the aluminum leg bands used to recognize individual birds. Their almost nonstop observations from 1 January 1933 through 15 February 1934 involved 197 mockingbirds. Eleven birds, residents or semiresidents around well-stocked feeders in their garden, provided most detailed information.

Both sets of researchers discovered that mockingbirds hold two types of territory. One is the summer or breeding territory which the normally monogamous pair holds jointly, and which the male actively defends as his mate settles down to egg-laying and incubation. Often, the male presents a number of nest sites from which the female selects one. Then he takes up most of the duties of nest building.

The second territory is a winter territory, usually smaller than the one the pair occupies in summer. Often, it is centered around a food source, usually a fruit-bearing tree or bush. In winter, a male may withdraw to a part of his old breeding territory and permit a female, often his previous mate, to occupy an adjacent portion. Both birds vigorously defend their winter territories against other mockingbirds and species such as robins, starlings, and woodpeckers who also compete for fruits. The intensity of defense may be linked, especially in cold weather, with securing an adequate supply of food.

The two clearly defined territories break down as seasons change. As the male begins to come into breeding condition he switches from winter to summer quarters, and establishes a nesting territory from about mid-January or early February onward. The female remains fairly subdued and is less mobile, staying in her winter area, until she selects a mate or, in the case of a previously paired bird, reunites with the male from the previous season. The other shift, from breeding to winter territory, takes place in late summer, usually from mid-August through mid-September, after adults have finished nesting and caring for young and have molted.

It is rare for territory holders to transgress on neighbors except when they pursue trespassing birds from the areas they defend into adjacent ones owned by other mockingbirds or when they assist neighbors to fight other species, or other members of their own species. The Micheners described ravenously hungry "wandering" mockingbirds raiding the territories of garden residents in early October in order to pilfer the ample supply of fruits on the feeders. Four or five resident mockers tackled these invaders, chasing them around the garden for many hours in an attempt to drive them away.

These loose aggregations of mobile adults and juveniles pose a constant threat to resident mockingbirds, who defend their winter territories with great vigor. Peter G. Merritt of Coral Gables, Florida, considered such acts of trespass to be coordinated so as to "swamp" a male defending a food source, in this case, a fig tree. He noted that dozens of northern mockers pecked at fruit in a large strangler fig after flying in from all directions. In doing so, most birds avoided the territorial male, who attempted to chase off birds as they arrived. Most mockingbirds succeeded in penetrating his defenses. Foraging by the group took place silently, as some mockingbirds consumed the ripe fruit in the tree, while others made off with it, probably to nearby territories. The mockingbird owner was unable to frustrate this strategy of feeding communally.

As the length of daylight increases and temperatures begin to rise, mockingbirds commence their songs. Both males and females sing, but the male's song medley is louder and is expressed more frequently. Initially they sing softly while hidden in shrubbery, but this "dream of song" grows louder until the male is carried away by long, voluminous cadences which he utters conspicuously from high perches. Mid-February in the American South is time for the mocker to initiate his song repertory, proclaiming his nesting territory. Soon he becomes a song zealot, flinging himself into the air, gliding along the boundaries of his chosen area in full voice, laying claim to the land. His aim is to attract a mate while warning off competing males.

As soon as a female enters his territory, the male challenges her with a series of harsh "chacks" or abrupt calls; the two birds square off and watch each other intently. The male pursues the female, and if she leaves he may try to entice her back with spread wings and soft calls. Once a pair bond is established, the ecstatic song bursts of the single, previously unattached male shift to shortened, more subdued cadences. Researchers characterize this in human terms as "happy, contented-sounding." Sitting together quietly both mockingbirds make a "hew-hew" call to keep in contact.

Laskey observed that some males sang more often than others, and that the same individual's song pattern shifted from one year to the next. In the first year, for example, until he found a mate, one mocker sang fully and excitedly in the inimitable way of the species. The next season, his mate from the year before returned in early March from an adjacent winter territory, just as the male started to sing. The "wild frenzy" of his song so characteristic of the previous year was curtailed. The two birds paired up again without belligerency and the male's song diminished as nesting activities began.

Cheryl A. Logan's work in Greensboro, North Carolina, indicates that a male's song serves to bring his mate into reproductive condition as well as to retain their breeding territory. Her study of six pairs of mockingbirds suggests that a brief burst of song produced during nest building may enhance the female's receptivity to mating. Unrestrained singing, either before fledglings have left the territory or with a nest failure due to predation or some other factor, "resets" the female's reproductive system.

The timing of song then appears important, for once a pair bond is established, song diminishes, occurring very infrequently after nestlings are hatched. Often the male may feed the fledglings while his mate begins a second clutch. If, however, this nest cycle is interrupted, the male will immediately begin to sing loudly. This outburst may lead some to condemn the mockingbird for apparent indifference over the loss of a nest and young only hours before. How could the species, it may be queried, be so blithe and forgetful after such a tragedy? An outpouring of song, however, may be a direct response to reproductive failure, as the male signals his mate for the nesting process to begin again.

Though the mockingbird is strongly monogamous, there are a few reported cases of bigamy. When a breeding male died in Guilford County, North Carolina, the already-mated neighboring male consorted with the female. By the close of the nesting period this male had initiated five nests with two females, out of which two clutches, both with his second mate, were raised to fledging. Biologists noted that the male shared duties with both females, but fed only the offspring of his second mate. Such "opportunistic bigamy," they concluded, led in this instance to greater reproductive success.

A second case of polygyny, or the mating of a male with more than one female, took place on the University of Miami campus at Coral Gables in 1984, and proved more complicated and puzzling. Two observers spent almost one hundred hours watching mocker no. 867, a color-banded male at least five years old, who bred with a second female occupying the portion of his territory away from the area still occupied by his first mate, with whom he had bred the previous year. Problems arose when no. 867 had two sets of young to feed. In one instance he fed only the fledglings of his first mate, leaving young birds in the second female's nest entirely for her to feed. At least one young bird died from starvation.

Male no. 867 changed strategies in the second nest overlap by initially feeding only his second mate's nestlings. He ignored his first mate's young, one of which died, possibly from starvation. He fed the second mate's youngsters until they fledged, then switched to his first female's emaciated nestlings, which gained weight rapidly with both parents feeding them. This switch back to younger siblings puzzled biologists, who are used to males assuming care of fledglings in monogamous situations.

"Supermocker" 867 veered from the norm in both mate selection and care of young. He was an unusually aggressive bird, fearless in attack, even to the point of striking people near his nest. He was tenacious in protection of his territory, and even defended mocker nests in adjacent territories. These singular qualities may well have attracted the second female to him. He consorted with both mates, but sang more frequently in the territory in which his first mate was established, suggesting a preference for that bird.

Supermocker departed from researchers' expectations by switching from feeding fledglings, which have at least some ability to forage, to feeding youngsters still in the nest. One unscientific explanation is that he learned from his mistake in the first overlap of young when he fed ony fledglings, leaving nestlings to starve. Observers suggest that male attention may be more important for nestlings than fledglings. In this instance, the result was a successful compromise, as half of his six nests with two mates produced independent young, better than the seasonal average for that part of Florida.

In 1985 on the University of North Carolina campus, a color-banded female raised six youngsters from four nesting attempts with two mates. This female had maintained a polyandrous relationship, that is, having more than one male at the same time, over several years, mating periodically with two males in adjacent territories. Both mates tolerated the female in their defended areas, and accepted her fledglings. Noting a biased sex ratio with males outnumbering females, observers concluded that male birds faced the choice of not breeding or accepting a mated female, and preferred the latter.

Many Northern Mockingbirds fail to find a mate. In fact, "Supermocker" went unpaired two seasons before practicing bigamy. If a male mockingbird fails to attract a mate, he will continue to sing loudly until late in the season, when he will abandon his territory. In some areas, notably North Carolina, unmated males may remain in a territory over a period of years without ever attracting a mate. In their Pasadena study, the Micheners describe how "Green" began to sing loudly after his mate, a one-legged mocker, was killed by a cat. "He began to sing incessantly as he had done before she came," they reported, "and this continued with scarcely a break for four days." Then Green gave up, and although very tame and habituated to feeding on raisins, he quit his territory and uncompleted nest, "flew off to the south, and we have never seen him since."

The sad episode had a sequel. Only two days after Green abandoned his territory in mid-May, another male took possession of it. "He sang all day and every day, and we thought at night as well," noted the California bird enthusiasts. "He seemed to delight in all the well-known antics of mockingbirds, flying up from his high perch and singing as he flew from tree to tree and filling the days with song as Green had done." This ardent singing continued for more than six weeks, but the new mocker failed to find a mate and left in early July. The Micheners heard no more singing that season, although other adult young mockingbirds foraged in the abandoned territory.

LAURA RILE

Nest, Eggs, and Young

*I*n Texas, mockingbirds lay their eggs from about the first week in March through late August, with April and May predominating. Arthur Cleveland Bent mentions similar dates for Florida, with a set of eggs found as early as March 3. Most mockers breed six to eight weeks later in South Carolina, although Bent lists nest building near Charleston on March 12, and a very late record for fledglings on September 10. California records show egg-laying continuing into late September.

Nest construction is a joint effort, lasting two or three days, but the male often does most of the work. Five or six nests may be built during the annual breeding period. The rather bulky structure is fashioned out of a platform of twigs upon which a compact mass of leaves, grasses, moss, hair, or artificial fibers is placed. The interior cup is lined with fine, soft rootlets, wool, or even bits of string. It holds a clutch of four eggs, less frequently three or five, rarely six, which are usually pale blue or green, blotched with russet or cinnamon.

Over the years Laskey noted that her mockingbirds in Nashville built in small evergreens (spruce, pine, boxwood, and especially cedar), but after deciduous plants put out leaves, nesting mockers favored them. Small hackberry trees, elms, locusts, and hawthorns predominated, but birds also used a variety of vines and privet-like shrubs.

Mockingbirds usually nest quite low, from about three feet to ten feet or less above the ground, although there are many exceptions. Laskey knew of a nest placed on exposed roots under an overhanging creek bank from which four young fledged. Other people have reported sites twenty feet up or more in trees. A bluebird nest box proved a most unusual site in Tennessee (in 1940); a ledge in a grape arbor, eaves under a wellhouse, and other human-made structures have also been used from time to time.

The areas around human habitations prove attractive for mockingbirds because they provide plenty of "edge," that is, a combination of plant cover and open space suitable for foraging and breeding. Gardens and subdivisions also offer a wide variety of berry-bearing plants upon which mockers depend. The density and height of grass cover in such places influence nesting success. A South Texas study by Roland R. Roth discovered that where herbaceous ground cover was short and sparse, mockers were able to snag insects successfully, retained territories after nest failures, and rebuilt, whereas in a similar area with a cover of longer, denser grass, the breeders tended to abandon their territories after nest failures.

The female incubates the clutch, starting after laying the last egg, while the male occupies a singing post, sometimes joining his mate when she feeds. Hatching occurs eleven to thirteen days after the beginning of incubation, and parents feed nestlings for about twelve days. The entire procedure of incubation and fledging approximates twenty-four days, varying between twenty-three and twenty-six days.

Both parents feed the young. Analysis of more than three thousand feeding journeys in Dade County, Florida, revealed that adults supplied food at similar rates, offering a mixed diet of animal and vegetable matter to their young. As the nestlings grew, males stepped up both the feeding tempo and the volume of food they carried in their beaks. Feeding rates peaked in the fifth and sixth days, just as the young were putting on weight most rapidly in the twelve-day cycle. In her studies, Laskey noted that there was enormous variation in the amount of time males gave to food procurement versus singing or nest defense. Usually, however, male mockingbirds play a major role in feeding the young after they leave the nest.

Amelia Laskey banded 904 young mockingbirds over a twenty-six-year period beginning in 1932, and she received information about 55, or 6 percent of them. Most reports, from a few weeks to five years after banding, came from the area in which an individual fledged. Five birds, however, turned up between 20 and 200 miles away. One was at Cumming, Georgia, 200 miles away, in April, one year and ten months after banding; another reached Fulton, Mississippi, 160 miles distant, in January, one year and eight months after banding; and a third, a year-old bird, was at Corinth, Mississippi, 128 miles southwest of Nashville. Immature birds wander in search of food and in order to establish their first territory, so it is not unusual for them to travel considerable distances. The Northern Mockingbird, however, is not as clearly migratory as other relatives. In a study of bird casualties against a television tower in Florida, Herbert L. Stoddard and Robert A. Norris characterized the species as a "night migrant," recording twenty-six deaths in eleven years, although its cousins the Brown Thrasher and Gray Catbird collided much more frequently with the obstacle when migrating at night.

Statistics from Laskey's Nashville study reveal that overall mockingbird fledging success (from nest initiation to free flying) was 56 percent, varying from 39 percent in early breeding attempts in March to 72 percent in July, when the number of nests built is significantly lower but may represent repeated breeding by experienced adults.

A North Carolina study showed how devastating inclement weather can be. J. Paul Visscher reported that many nests situated in yuccas were frequently destroyed by torrential rains. He discovered several nests in ruins after storms; others filled up with water and the young drowned.

Hawks, kestrels, cats, jays, crows, raccoons, opossums, snakes—Audubon's painting showed three mockingbirds battling with a snake about to pilfer eggs in the nest—and of course, humans, are threats to breeding mockingbirds. A 1980–1981 Louisiana study by William T. Joern and James F. Jackson noted that birds and snakes (kingsnakes, racers, ratsnakes) proved most destructive, taking eggs, nestlings, and adults. A Texas ratsnake 102 centimeters long regurgitated an adult female mockingbird after humans captured it. The eggs in the nest disappeared within three days after observers set the snake free. The authors speculated that nests placed in isolated patches of vegetation suffered less predation than those in continuous strips because snakes are less likely to leave the extensive cover of fence rows, for example, in order to hunt in shrubs separated by grassy openings.

It is widely assumed, though difficult to prove, that while engaged in food gathering and courtship, birds in general are more vulnerable to predation. Predators seize unsuspecting or distracted individuals and their progeny. Slightly more than one-third of eggs laid in the middle latitudes by species like the Northern Mockingbird are filched by mammals, reptiles, and other birds. Perching mockingbirds are likely to catch sight of predators more easily than those engaged in other duties. Nearby mockers pick up alarm squawks quickly and often join in vigorous attacks on intruders. Aggression shown toward cats, Blue Jays, and humans is proverbial. In fact mail carriers in a Houston neighborhood refused to deliver letters due to assaults by aggressive mockers. The U.S. Postal Service received *Texas Monthly*'s "Bum Steer Award" in February 1986 for its timidity.

Young mockingbirds disperse after they have fledged. It was at this time that Amelia Laskey observed "wing-flashing," or wing-raising from young birds on the ground. There is much speculation about the reasons for this rather odd behavior. Laskey and others have argued that it seems an involuntary re-action to a new or strange object. "The approach is slow and halting," she wrote in a 1962 article in *The Auk;* "the wings are slowly raised . . . horizontally or upward, sometimes alter-nately as the bird peers at a certain spot or object." Noted orni-thologist and bird artist George M. Sutton agreed that wing-flashing, or "spreading the wings archangel-fashion" as he put it, is an instinctive gesture, associated more or less tangentially with the procurement of food. Others argue that wing-flashing surprises insects, making them easier to spot and capture on or near the ground.

Texas-based ornithologists Robert K. Selander and K. D. Hunter observed this wing-flashing display directed at a screech owl in a live oak tree on the University of Texas campus in Aus-tin. They counted sixteen wing-flashes in ten minutes in adult mockingbirds mobbing the owl, and decided to place a dummy owl and photograph its effects on mockers. They concluded that wing-flashing is innate behavior, practiced by fledglings and even by nestlings. It is a characteristic of wariness or suspi-cion which has acquired the secondary significance of helping toward food-gathering.

Song

*T*he merits of the Northern Mockingbird's song have been hotly contested in pages of both popular and professional journals. Cage bird fanciers liked the rather dull-colored mockingbird because it sang so well. Nature authors such as John Burroughs preferred the rough and ready ways of European perching birds—they adapted better to humanized landscapes, he argued. But he loved the mocker's exuberance and versatility, discussing the respective merits of this species versus the nightingale.

Two aspects of mockingbird vocalization demand attention. The first is the character of the song itself which birds deliver for a good three-fourths of the year. The second is the bird's special powers of mimicry, that is, its ability to imitate the songs and calls of other species, including sounds made by less highly regarded animals such as chickens, frogs, and crickets, and even machines like saws and pumps. A mockingbird may imitate the calls, songs, or song phrases of over thirty bird species, including that of the Red-winged Blackbird, which cannot distinguish between its own song and the mocker's imitation of it. Boston's famous "Arnold Arboretum" bird, who turned up in November 1914 and sang powerfully on and off for more than five and a half years, was credited with imitations of fifty-one species. Although other birds have shown a proclivity to copy sounds, none has attracted quite as much attention as North America's own comedian—the mockingbird.

One expert on bird songs, Donald J. Borror, concludes that most species in the Mimidae family are accomplished songsters. Although the loudness, pitch, and quality of phrases vary among species, mockingbird, thrasher, and catbird songs are sustained and express a large variety of phrases. The Northern Mockingbird's song resembles that of the Gray Catbird and Brown Thrasher in terms of phrase changes and the protracted length of time a single bird may spend in song. However, the mockingbird, says Borror, is more musical, with fewer discordant or jarring notes, and tends to be more repetitive. A male will sound a phrase several times in succession before changing over to a new one, and within that phrase there may be several notes that sound like other species. This copying of other birds' calls and songs is more characteristic of mockingbirds in the northern portions of their range. One plausible explanation is that as the density of mockingbirds decreases, the opportunity to hear and learn from each other also decreases, so that individuals are forced to copy the notes of other species.

Where does all this sound come from and what does it mean? The physiology of bird song centers on the syrinx, the voice-box of birds, analogous to the larynx in mammals. This chamber at the base of the trachea or windpipe forks into bronchial tubes leading to the lungs and air sacs. The syrinx is a series of cartilaginous rings joined by connective tissue, and the most common type forms a box-like structure varying in musculature according to the musical range of the species. Most true songbirds such as the mockingbird have five to nine, usually seven, pairs of syrinx muscles, which act rather like a trumpet in controlling the passage of air from the interior across elastic membranes which are stretched beside the openings between the bronchial tubes and windpipe. Tension in the membranes defines voice pitch, while the windpipe itself acts as a resonator to dampen or enhance the timbre of song. The amount of membrane vibration within the syrinx produces the quality of song that characterizes the species.

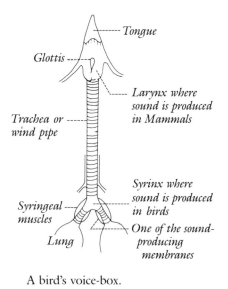

A bird's voice-box.

Based on Arthur A. Allen,
The Book of Bird Life, 2d ed.
(New York: Van Nostrand, 1961).

Sound conveys rapid, varied, and subtle signals in animals, including humans. For many creatures, a call note, song, or other vocalization reveals the subject's identity, location, mood, or predisposition. Birds and insects live in a world of sounds. Birds such as mockingbirds, which gather food habitually on or near the ground, often concealed from each other by dense vegetation, produce high-quality songs, though often, oddly enough, also harsh and grating calls.

The Northern Mockingbird learns to sing by listening to fellow mockers toward which it is predisposed. Individual birds develop their full song repertoires while practicing their vocal abilities by copying various sounds, usually the songs of other birds but in some circumstances other animal or mechanical noises. This copying of sound presupposes an innate, flexible capacity for producing songs. By putting in the song phrases and calls of other birds the mockingbird may discourage potential competition. In this way song imitation has value for survival; it also may break up monotony and repetition. Philosopher Charles A. Hartshorne, a life-long student of birds, also argues that it becomes an "identity tag" for individual birds who are recognizable by their specific imitations. But Hartshorne notes that the mocker's loose musical style reflects a limited sense of musicality:

A Mockingbird takes a phrase out of the variable sequence of the Wood Thrush, simplifies even this phrase (in all cases which I have heard), and either repeats it immediately two or more times (which is quite contrary to Wood Thrush practice and musical spirit) or passes immediately to something different and musically rather irrelevant. In either case he misses the main musical point of the song, which is the eliciting of exquisitely harmonic contrasts between the successive phrases in the sequence, these phrases being both deeply contrasting and musically related. Far more adequate is the Mockingbird's rendering of the Carolina Wren; somewhat more adequate, his version of the Cardinal.

This imitative ability demonstrates neither fondness for musical pattern nor purity. The mocker is a medleyist, concludes Hartshorne, using snatches of what other birds compose.

Enthusiasts would probably disagree; so would William H. Hudson, Argentine-born nature author based in England, who penned what is possibly the greatest tribute to any bird—the White-banded Mockingbird (*Mimus triurus*)—for its song genius and the quality of its imitations. Writing for a British audience, Hudson likened the white-banded's song to that of the European skylark but noted that this South American mockingbird has more power, joyousness, and abandon. It possesses "endless variations and [is] brightened and spiritualized in a degree that cannot be imagined," he exclaimed. No other species could emulate this "divine song," and few had its abilities to imitate the songs of other birds, some of which never visit Patagonia, where Hudson first heard it.

Hartshorne, in acknowledging Hudson's eulogy, calls *M. triurus* the "best migrant imitator," but suggests that the Old World Bluethroat and Marsh Warbler imitate almost as well, and a score of Australasian birds are renowned for mimicry. He does, however, place the White-banded Mockingbird high among the world's superior singers, listing it with six other *Mimus* species, including our own Northern Mockingbird.

If singing skill is enhanced by characteristics of territoriality, dullness of plumage, and feeding on or near the ground, as some experts suggest, then our mockingbird fits these parameters perfectly. By its powerful, sustained song the male proclaims his gender, establishes a territory, attracts a mate, and synchronizes breeding behavior. There is, however, disagreement about whether song is important in maintaining a territory and in keeping out intruders. Mockers do not defend a territory with song in the sense of singing as they chase out a trespasser.

Socially, song identifies the species, and calls convey information about enemies or dangerous situations. Mimicry may possibly enable a particular bird to exclude from its territory members of the species whose song it imitates. Mockingbird song probably serves to identify one individual to another and perhaps satisfies or fulfills that individual's commitment to life. This is an unscientific observation, but the complexity, duration, and enormous amount of energy and attention which many Northern Mockingbirds give to singing seem to argue against our attempts to deprive them of emotions.

Cage Birds and Conservationists

"When taken from the nest, the 'prince of musicians' becomes a contented captive, and has been known to live many years in confinement," said ornithologist and army surgeon Elliott Coues (1842–1899), putting forward the mocker's best qualities of docility, hardiness, and relative longevity. Such a "feathered musician," America's nightingale, compared favorably in many people's opinions with the celebrated, inspirational *Luscinia megarhyncha*, or true Nightingale, from the Old World, which is related to the thrushes and chats. Caged mockingbirds, like nightingales, could fill the house or garden aviary with strong, joyous sound, causing heads to turn and becoming graceful, interesting, and even playful companions. The mockingbird was easier to raise in captivity than the Old World nightingale and might live for upward of half a dozen years.

Bird authority Alexander Wilson (1766–1813) recognized that those mockingbirds taken "rather young than otherwise" did best in captivity. The idea was to stake out a nest and remove the young after they were well grown so that they took homemade foods readily and adjusted quickly to the loss of their parents. Wilson recommended a milk-based corn mash spiced with red meat and fruit. Other diets included hard-boiled eggs and potato mash, all kinds of berries, especially huckleberries, and insects; spiders especially strengthened young birds and cured sick individuals. European fanciers supplied their North American charges with thrush-type foods, hand-rearing youngsters, whom "feckless" parents frequently abandoned, on egg yolk, lean meat, beetles, and fruit. A balanced diet made it relatively easy to raise *M. polyglottos* in captivity.

Getting adults to nest successfully proved more difficult, partly because one had to be ingenious or just lucky to find a male and female, for gender markings are extremely subtle, and partly because the mockingbird proved pugnacious and could disrupt other passerines in the aviary, taxing the aviculturist's patience and forbearance.

The Reverend C. D. Farrar, sometime scholar of University

College, Durham, and vicar of Micklefield, Leeds, Yorkshire, received considerable recognition from British aviculturists for his success with mockingbirds. He recalled that it took him four years to breed his American charges because "I tried valiantly to breed from two cocks." He had read all the columns and instructions about the species, but only determined the male gender of his two birds after a serious fight in which one of them lost an eye. "The only way that I could see was to get half-a-dozen Mockingbirds together and compare them." He failed. "Some of them had more white on the wing; some were lighter, some darker; but I felt sure they were cocks by their build and carriage," complained the clergyman. Finally, in desperation Farrar began to examine their eye color and found among a big lot of mockingbirds two with green eyes—"for with the green eye there went a general look of femininity," he exclaimed. His hunch worked. After he released a green-eyed bird with his one-eyed male, the pair soon commenced to build a "warmly lined" nest in an elder bush. Ignoring companion titmice, bulbuls, quail, and blackcaps, the mockers hatched out two young, fed them on mealworms, and when they fledged, the male sang magnificently, "proud, I suppose, of his success," concluded Farrar.

In the tradition of parson-naturalist, Farrar took a keen interest in birds. He penned two books and a number of articles about caged bird management, and included his experience with the mockingbird in the humorously titled *Through a Bird-Room Window*. Before ill-health forced Farrar to give up bird-keeping, the expert aviculturist claimed a British record of having reared from nest and eggs no fewer than twenty-four different birds. In addition to the mockingbird, Farrar's other American successes included the Gray Catbird, Indigo Bunting, and Painted Bunting.

Another Britisher, A. G. Butler, who devoted thirty-two years to maintaining an aviary, also kept and bred mockingbirds, but found them "mischievous" owing to the "pleasure which they took in scaring their associates." The antics of these American birds proved fascinating, however, and made up for their comparatively nondescript plumage. In general, British

bird fanciers discovered that mockingbirds were easily tamed but difficult to breed. German aviculturists, who utilized the regimen of potato, egg, fruit, and live food, did better. One of them at Weimar reportedly reared sixty Northern Mocking-birds in ten years.

American bird keepers appear to have experienced similar difficulties with mockingbirds. One connoisseur acknowledged the problem of distinguishing between sexes. He relied on the "four-feather" principle, which held that a perfectly marked bird with clear white half-moon markings on the four primary feathers nearest the tip of the wing is invariably a male, whereas "white color on the feathers of the female bird will be found to be splashed, and irregularly marked throughout." In truth, however, a great deal of variation occurs in the shape and amount of white on the primaries, and so it is not a reliable guide in distinguishing the sexes.

Another issue surrounding the keeping of mockingbirds centered on their songs and abilities to mimic other birds, domesticated animals, and even sounds made by farm implements. Early-nineteenth-century bird expert Alexander Wilson argued that "the best singing birds . . . are those that have been reared in the country," learning from conspecifics and from other songbirds a whole range of natural sounds. One enthusiast taught a hand-reared bird to sing by placing an older individual close by so that captivity did not limit the bird's repertoire.

Thomas Nuttall (1786–1859), another nineteenth-century English birdman and noted botanist, picking up this theme of song and mimicry, drew heavily from Wilson. Nuttall, a York-shireman, argued that so skillful were a mocker's imitations that even sportsmen could be deceived into thinking quail, doves, or other game species were close. Captivity dulled neither the polyglot's song nor its vitality. An individual "often becomes familiar with his master; playfully attacks him through the bars of his cage, or at large in a room; restless and capricious, he seems to try every expedient of a lively imagination that may conduce to his amusement," remarked the bemused Nuttall.

Not all were so supportive or so entertained by mockingbird antics. Britisher W. T. Greene, author of *Birds I Have Kept in Years Gone By* (1885), qualified his regard for Northern Mockingbirds by insisting disdainfully that "we who are accustomed to hear the Nightingale, the Blackcap and the Thrush, are compelled to demur" against American claims about the high quality of song. He did not hold the opinion that the mockingbird was the best songster of all cage birds, perhaps because hand-reared birds lacked the wild bird's song. Greene admitted that as a cage species the mockingbird had "some merit" because it was hardy, although not to "be trusted in a mixed aviary." In another book, entitled *Favourite Foreign Birds for Cages and Aviaries,* Greene reported that "the insignificant-looking grey bird" had "frequently bred in confinement," although others noted that it nested rather uncommonly.

There were times, however, when the usually feisty bird showed signs of dyspepsia. Wilson and others suggested "a few spiders" to cure the malaise. Others plying the bird trade took a more meticulous stance. Poultry expert George Burnham had two concerns about keeping mockingbirds: proper feeding and cage hygiene. Like domestic fowl, mockers sometimes developed "pip," the habit of sneezing as if to remove something from the mouth. A blunt knife or fingernail scraped against the tip of the tongue usually removed the hard substance. Spiders, a dozen daily, kept the bird from being sluggish or dumpy, and iron from a rusty nail in its drink addressed diarrhea. Kerosene in the cage regularly removed lice, and a touch under its wings and vent killed any of them on a mocker's body. Prevention was Burnham's hallmark. By keeping bird cages clean and captives properly fed, bird fanciers were guaranteed pleasure and satisfaction.

The delights of keeping cage birds as promoted by Burnham and various avicultural groups, numbering about two hundred in Europe and America in 1880, reached a zenith in the closing decades of the nineteenth century. True bird "fancying" peaked in Germany, where aviculturists constructed entire bird rooms for exotic species. *The Illustrated Book of Canaries and Cage-Birds* by W. A. Blakston, W. Swaysland, and August F. Wiener

(London, n.d.), acknowledged that Germany "has more foreign birds [which] are kept and bred there than in the rest of
Europe together." There were as many societies in Germany as
in the United States, and they were supported by aristocrats
like the Crown Prince of Austria. Much of this popularity
stemmed from the articles of a certain Karl Russ who promoted cage bird raising in Berlin during the late 1860s and
early 1870s.

Russ selected the North American mockingbird as "the most
excellent of all songsters." In listening attentively to its song,
one heard "Nature's own music," he declared. No songbird
could equal the mellowness, modulations, compass, or execution of the mockingbird. The nightingale was able to equal the
species on occasion, but did not possess the "finished talent"
which made the American bird so appealing.

At home in the United States, museum custodian and ornithologist Henry Nehrling was unhappy about carelessness in
keeping this popular caged songster. "With many people it is a
mere fashion to keep a Mockingbird," he complained. They
take nestlings, leave the cage outdoors so that adults feed them,
then neglect the fledglings. He noted that "great cargoes" of
young entered the markets of Chicago and New York in mid-
June, selling for five dollars apiece. Survivors sold as adults for
as much as twenty-five dollars, and still found ready buyers.
But there was a great loss, and most died because of mistreat-
ment or ignorance.

During the final quarter of the nineteenth century, as popular interest in cage birds grew, more and more people began to
question bird traffic and aviary building for two basic reasons.
First, the declining numbers of many species, particularly useful ones, due to their exploitation for the meat and millinery
trades and for the cage bird fad, gave rise to a debate over human rights and duties toward the natural world and its wild
creatures. It was clear that the myth of superabundance, by
which people judged it impossible to make a substantial dent
in wild mammal or bird populations, was indeed a chimera.
Populations of bison, passenger pigeons, elk, pronghorn, deer,
waterfowl, and shorebirds in North America dropped pre-

cipitously, alarming sportsmen and scientists, who began organizing campaigns to conserve wildlife.

Sportsman George Bird Grinnell's "Audubon Society," founded in the pages of *Forest and Stream* (11 February 1886), drew attention to the slaughter of birds to provide ornamental feathers for stylish hats and bonnets. Mockingbirds, together with scores of other passerine species, plus larger herons, pelicans, and even albatrosses, were falling in large numbers to the guns and nets set out by millinery agents. The Audubon movement sounded the call for bird appreciation and bird study in order to determine how various species contributed to the "balance of nature." One aim of this movement was to press various state legislatures to legally distinguish game birds from nongame birds, and to protect the latter year round. The "Model Law," promoted by the Audubon Society and by the American Ornithologists' Union (founded in 1884), listed beneficial and harmless species, including the mocker, and differentiated them from pests. As state after state adopted the Model Law's provisions, nongame birds received sufficient help for many species to recover.

In addition to the spectre of extinction due to overhunting and continued exploitation, there was the second but complementary issue of cruelty, which more directly affected the traffic in live birds. A glimpse of conditions in nineteenth-century city bird markets comes from French nature enthusiast Jules Michelet, who wrote a popular, widely read book, *The Bird,* in the late 1860s. The Marché Saint Germain in Paris was a great market for birds. Walking among the various stalls heaped with cages comprising a "strange museum of French ornithology" proved a heart-wrenching experience for Michelet. Especially touching, in the Frenchman's eyes, were the mockingbirds, whose unique "comedian's genius" enabled them to mimic the character and songs of the other birds with a certain irony. These foreigners formed part of the army of winged slaves waiting to be auctioned. Michelet saw finches blinded by having their eyelids sewn together. He noted how some birds crashed against bars in a bloodied frenzy; how others seemed resigned to captivity, or appeared broken and listless. He caught in the gleam of yet other birds' eyes a look that seemed to implore, "Buy me, buy me!" The whole bustling, sordid market sickened Michelet; the presence of America's mockingbird was a bright spot in the otherwise sad scene, "an orchestra in himself," he said, capable of giving expression to his own song as well as copying the songs of others.

Keeping foreign birds unable to subsist in new lands to which people transported them, or semi-domesticated species like canaries and pigeons, as pets was a more or less acceptable tradition, but as the young century progressed, more and more people in this country agreed that native American birds were more appropriately observed out of doors in their own haunts, not in aviaries. State and federal legislation made it illegal for the general public to keep wild birds as pets. One of the reasons, apart from protecting useful species which helped to keep down agricultural pests, focused on cruelty. New sentiments likened bear-baiting and dog fighting to a decline in civic and social virtues; caging birds was likewise seen as brutish behavior, unworthy of the cherished American values of individual freedom and compassion for the weak. In the last two decades or so the traffic in foreign species has also become more restricted as efforts to stamp out declines abroad as well as at home have led to laws curbing the import of live birds.

The tendency to apply human qualities to bird behavior— talking about "affectionate" flycatchers, swallows so "assiduous" in raising their young, etc.—helped oddly enough to make the universe appear less human-centered. These creatures had the right to pursue their own lives of undoubted virtue without being confined or held captive for purposes of human vanity or display. Bird protectionists inveighed against bird killing (the alien House Sparrow proved an embarrassment in this regard) and against bird capture.

For a subscription of one dollar per year, the Audubon Society's bi-monthly *Bird-Lore,* launched by American Museum of Natural History ornithologist Frank M. Chapman and supported by educators, popular writers, and fellow scientists, promised to popularize bird study and conservation. A section for "Teachers and Students" helped to identify more common garden birds and to explain their habits, including those of the Northern Mockingbird. "Mockingbird Notes," in an early issue (1901), included information and photographs about the bird's nesting cycle in Baldwin, Louisiana. *Cassinia,* the publication of the Delaware Valley Ornithological Club of Philadelphia, carried a note about the distribution of the species in the same year, while "The Mocking Bird at Home" appeared in 1902 in *The Osprey,* another illustrated, popular journal published in Washington, D.C.

These and other popular journals heaped accolades upon the mockingbird and called attention to the birds as individuals. A 1906 article in *Bird-Lore* described the life of "Sir Roger de Coverley," a five-year-old mockingbird who lived in a garden in Port Orange, Florida. Mabel Osgood Wright, author and active Audubon Society promoter, included "dem Mockers" in *Gray Lady and the Birds* (1907). In this tale a black cook from the South instructs a boy, who has brought a caged mocker into her kitchen, about the character, song, and confiding ways of the gray bird. The mistress of the house, "Gray Lady," permits him to keep the bird until spring because it is injured; nevertheless, she instructs the young lad never to confine wild birds in cages as the practice thwarts nature's designs and causes needless suffering. Wright's point was that the mockingbird is so unusually "winning and sociable in its relations with man" that it should always remain unmolested. That such "friendliness is ill rewarded by the theft of its nestlings, that they may be sold at home and abroad" was, in her eyes, most regrettable.

The Mockingbird
in American Culture

Birds have served as ornaments and symbols for as long as humans have admired their appearance and behavior. We have beautified our bodies with bird feathers. We have conjured the powers and nobility of birds into badges denoting status and authority. The Bald Eagle is a prime example; for over two hundred years it has symbolized America's sense of power, courage, and nobility. We regard this species, like ourselves, as bold and fearless, despite Ben Franklin's view that is is a cowardly bird, one that prefers eating dead fish and carrion to seeking live prey.

During the colonial period only a few American authors mentioned birds at all, and most of them ignored *Mimus polyglottos.* This neglect extended through the revolutionary period, although natural historian William Bartram noted the mockingbird's habit of jumping up in song—as if to "recover or recall his very soul, expired in the last elevated strain." In his *Travels,* a 1770s narrative of a trip through the Carolinas, Georgia, and Florida, Bartram idealized the mockingbird. In an idyll of pastoral contentment in the South, he referred to the landscape of rice plantations and corn patches interspersed with palms and laurels that conveyed variety and contentment to the eye. Days and entire nights in that lovely place reverberated to "the melody of the cheerful mockingbird, warbling nonpareil, and plaintive turtle dove." He discovered the gray mocker to be alert, merry, and active—"vocal and joyous, [it] mounts aloft on silvered wings, rolls over and over, then gently descends and presides in the choir of tuneful tribes."

In this way, this bird fitted the romantic image of the American South as a semitropical paradise appropriately planted with Mediterranean orchards and gardens. The mockingbird's unequaled voice reverberated throughout a landscape flooded with sunlight and balmy air. According to John Hanson, it expresses the spirit of place in the South as "the incarnate sport of the climate, the voice of the realm trying to give utterance to the feelings of the flowers, the mountains, valleys and all the voiceless things."

As the nineteenth century progressed, the mockingbird's joyous song, bustling ways, and boldness attracted more and more writers. James Fenimore Cooper thought its song the equal of any European songbird's. Henry David Thoreau rarely mentioned the mockingbird because it was not common in his New England haunts, but New Yorker John Burroughs, more widely traveled than Thoreau, became a mockingbird devotee. Burroughs believed that the distribution of this species affected its literary appreciation. He maintained that "if poets were as plentiful down South as they are in New England, we should have heard of this song long ago, and had it celebrated in appropriate verse."

STEVEN HOLT / VIREO

Walt Whitman's "Out of the Cradle Endlessly Rocking" represents the mockingbird song with unmatched power. In the poem, a boy discovers the nest of a visiting mockingbird pair— "guests from Alabama, two together"—beside the Long Island shore where he lives. Throughout the spring, the boy watches the pair as they make their new home far from southern climes:

> Till of a sudden,
> May-be killed, unknown to her mate,
> One forenoon the she-bird crouched not on the nest,
> Nor returned that afternoon, nor the next,
> Nor ever appeared again.
>
> And thenceforward all summer in the sound of the sea,
> And at night under the full of the moon in calmer weather,
> Over the hoarse surging of the sea,
> Or flitting from brier to brier by day,
> I saw, I heard at intervals the remaining one, the he-bird,
> The solitary guest from Alabama.
>
> *Blow! blow! blow!*
> *Blow up sea-winds along Paumanok's shore;*
> *I wait and I wait till you blow my mate to me.*
>
> Yes, when the stars glistened,
> All night long on the prong of a moss-scallop'd stake,
> Down almost amid the slapping waves,
> Sat the lone singer wonderful causing tears.
>
> He called on his mate,
> He poured forth the meaning which I of all men know.

Whitman's feel for the pulse of life, his sense of personal loneliness and deep need for reassurance and love surface through the mockingbird, which strains to catch a replying whisper from its lost mate only to have hopes dashed:

> *That is the whistle of the wind, it is not my voice,*
> *That is the fluttering, the fluttering of the spray,*
> *Those are the shadows of leaves.*
>
> *O darkness! O in vain!*
> *O I am very sick and sorrowful.*

"Out of the Cradle" is a profound example of bird symbol in American letters. Whitman exalts the human virtue of hope in his treatment of the mockingbird. Faced with the sudden loss of its mate, the survivor begins a vigil, singing for his loved one and straining to detect a response against the timeless ocean's roar. The mockingbird lives in hope. Like faith, hope springs from within the individual and sustains him within emotional turmoil and an indifferent universe. The mocker is steadfast. Hope sustains his life and inspires love.

Tradition held that Southern birds sang best, and Burroughs argued that nocturnal refrains, admired by Whitman and associated by Burroughs with the lark and nightingale, were worth the trip south to hear. One southern poet, Richard Henry Wilde, although deriding the bird, celebrated the mocker's song:

> Winged mimic of the woods! thou motley fool,
> Who shall thy gay buffonery describe?
> Thine ever-ready notes of ridicule
> Pursue thy fellows still with jest and jibe.
> Wit—sophist—songster—Yorick of thy tribe,
> Thou sportive satirist of nature's school,
> To thee the palm of scoffing we ascribe,
> Arch scoffer and mad Abbot of misrule!
> For such thou art by day—but all night long
> Thou pour'st a soft, sweet, pensive, solemn strain . . .

Such "soft, sweet, pensive" strains "coming from Nature's own musician" aroused in some nostalgic feelings for the American South. Bird artist John James Audubon, for instance, longed for a glimpse of magnolia woods, a thousand perfumed flowers, and the "mellow Mock-bird, or Wood-thrush" in order to relieve his homesickness during dreary winter days in England. Louisiana was for Audubon a treasure trove of natural wonders. "It is where Nature seems to have paused, as she passed over the earth," he claimed, "and opening her stores, to have strewed with unsparing hand the diversified seeds from which have sprung all the beautiful and splendid forms which I should in vain attempt to describe, that the

Mockingbird should have fixed its abode, there only that its wondrous song should be heard."

Audubon's famous *The Birds of America* regards the mockingbird as a huge butterfly flitting effortlessly among evergreens and many-hued blossoms. One bird circles around another in courtship and pours out a melody of which the "varied modulations and gradations, the extent of its compass, the great brilliancy of execution are unequaled." This "king of song" had no equals; certainly no bird in the British Isles could match the mockingbird's song medley.

The mockingbird seemed to be most vocal and self-confident in the South. Henry Nehrling penned a handsome two-volume book titled *Our Native Birds of Song and Beauty* (1893), noting in it how this trim, gray-colored songster sought out human settlements, especially those "beautiful southern gardens." Nowhere were they as common, declared Nehrling, as on the farms and in gardens—from Florida's citrus groves all the way westward to every large garden in the city of Houston, Texas.

Harper Lee's famous novel, *To Kill a Mockingbird* (1960), is quintessentially southern in content and scope. The mockingbird symbol works on several levels. First, the bird is a creature over which humans have unfair advantage; we are morally obliged, therefore, to exercise restraint in our dealings with it. When giving an air rifle to his son, the narrator's father, Atticus, tells the boy to shoot "at tin cans in the yard, but I know you'll go after birds. Shoot all the bluejays you want, if you can hit 'em, but remember it's a sin to kill a mockingbird." The sin, explains a neighbor, is to murder harmless creatures that "don't do one thing but sing their hearts out for us." The Blue Jay, noted more for bullying ways, is presumably expendable.

On another level, cruelty to the mockingbird is analogous to the unjust treatment and later murder of a black man, Tom Robinson, who is falsely charged with rape, and then lynched. Robinson gets into trouble by trying to help someone weaker and more vulnerable. The mockingbird represents the victims of racism in the South. Thus, in addition to using the mockingbird as a nostalgic symbol of her childhood, Lee employs it as a metaphor to attack racial injustice and human cruelty.

In his recent novel entitled *Mockingbird* (1980), Walter Tevis, like Whitman, uses the species as a metaphor for human hope. A phrase, "only the mockingbird sings from the edge of the woods," occupies the mind and awakens dormant emotions in a man and woman rebelling in a future world controlled by machines. The story's human protagonists assume the mockingbird's characteristics. They search for new horizons from the "wood" of programmed existence. Mockingbird song expresses their own emancipatory yearning for culture long suppressed, especially for those qualities of compassion, trust, and sharing that humans possess. Whereas Whitman places emphasis on the quality of steadfastness in his love-lorn mocker, Tevis uses the image of the same bird to reunite a human couple. The woodland minstrel is the harbinger of happiness and fulfillment rather than of deprivation and loss.

Other authors draw upon the mockingbird for ironic counterpoint. In Ford Madox Ford's *The Good Soldier* (1915), for example, a main character, wealthy John Dowell, elopes one night with Florence Hurlbird against her family's wishes. The couple pass the remaining hours before dawn in a wood, "listening to a mocking-bird imitate an old tom cat." The older man fails to recognize either his own impotence or his new wife's sexual profligacy; it is for the reader to discern in the mockingbird's tomcat imitation a comment upon Dowell's—and all of the novel's major characters'—sexual incompetence.

Audubon depicts mockingbirds fending off a rattlesnake
—an unrealistic situation since rattlesnakes are not known
to climb trees or attack birds.

State Birds

Author Shirley A. Briggs has aptly stated that few state birds "would seem at home on a banner waving over a battlefield." State birds are generally species that appeal because of their colors, melodious songs, and confiding ways; they occur commonly around homes and gardens. Some of them were selected more or less by accident or as reminders of historic events and regional characteristics. Alabama's "yellowhammer," or Yellow-shafted Flicker, became the state bird because its markings resemble the uniform of the old cavalry. The Rhode Island Red, a domestic chicken, supported by poultry interests, won out in that state because conservationists, school children, and others split their votes among several native bird species.

In general, however, state birds, like state flowers and trees, are species that are well known, well liked, and widely distributed. The Cardinal thus holds primary place in seven states; the Western Meadowlark, denizen of open, exposed grasslands, represents six plains and western states; while the Mockingbird, typifying the fecundity, sunlight, and luxuriance of the Old South, is officially enshrined by five states—Arkansas, Florida, Mississippi, Tennessee, and Texas. It almost became South Carolina's choice as well but lost out to the appropriately named Carolina Wren.

Henry Nehrling suggested that as pioneers transformed the landscapes of southern states, the mockingbird attached itself to humans; it nested within a few feet of crude cabins, on rail fences, flitting around open areas with consummate agility and boldness. For many others, too, the mockingbird symbolizes the pioneer spirit, capturing a sense of self-assertion and individualism. Texas naturalist Roy Bedichek admired this characteristic most about the bird. "He is indomitable," Bedichek declared, remembering how a pair in his yard "worked like beavers" in a drought to rear young successfully when other species had given up. "They fought it out" by standing up to harsh conditions, not buckling under.

Rugged behavior conquered the frontier of Arkansas, Tennessee, and Texas. Bedichek found the mocker to be intolerant of "carpet-bagger" robins; it attacked them and even menacing rattlesnakes with ruthless audacity. He is "out of temper with other birds generally and testy at every trespass," Bedichek noted, seeing in that gloomy amber eye and slightly downward bill the intense look of a hawk. "He is ever too full of business, too downright, too intense, to be merry," he concluded, finding dourness, not merriment to be the hallmark of the species.

The mockingbird's spread represents the pioneering concept most literally. Opportunistically taking over cleared areas around towns and farms in wooded regions, the mockingbird

STATE RECOGNITION	
Texas	Senate Concurrent Resolution No. 8, by the Federation of Women's Clubs *31 January 1927*
Florida	Senate Concurrent Resolution No. 3, supported by Audubon Societies *22 April 1927*
Arkansas	House Concurrent Resolution No. 22, supported by the Federation of Women's Clubs *5 March 1929*
Tennessee	Senate Joint Resolution No. 51, supported by Tennessee Ornithological Society, Garden Clubs, PTAs, etc. *19 April 1933*
Mississippi	Proposed by Federation of Women's Clubs as avian emblem in 1929 *Official Recognition, 1944*

also expanded its range into the more barren west as settlers planted trees about their residences. There is a record for colonization of Lubbock, Texas, in 1932 from brushlands in the east below the Caprock escarpment. Mockingbird arrivals coincided with tree and shrub planting within the growing city limits.

Many people believed that the mocker both tolerated and sought out human companionship by choosing to live in and around new settlements. When authorities urged citizens to take an interest in nature, they celebrated this species because of its confiding and pioneer ways. It was a bird people had come to know. Conservation-oriented groups, most notably the General Federation of Women's Clubs, spearheaded campaigns to select state birds. Women's associations gave clout to this cause because they were committed to landscape beautification and to educating the public, notably school children, about the aesthetic and useful qualities of birds. The choice of a species, therefore, normally rested upon the public's familiarity and liking for it. Campaigns for state birds were good for wildlife conservation, and with sponsor support, legislatures and governors acted quickly to designate popular choices.

In November 1926, the 50,000-member Texas Federation of Women's Clubs, through its Birds, Flowers, and Garden Division, nominated the mockingbird as state bird. Mrs. Howard Hicks and Mrs. L. A. Wells placed their resolution before the federation's assembly in Dallas, which then passed it along to the state legislature in January 1927. To garner support, these women asked local clubs to have a vote taken in public schools on the issue. On January 31, the legislature unanimously adopted a resolution proclaiming the mocker as the most appropriate species:

. . . it is found in all parts of the State, in winter and in summer, in the city and in the country, on the prairie and in the woods and hills, and is a singer of distinctive type, a fighter for the protection of his home, falling, if need be, in its defense, like any true Texan . . .

Governor Dan Moody signed the resolution the same day.

In Florida officials were less impressed by the mockingbird's heroic character than by its "matchless charm," especially in its music. They agreed with birdman Arthur H. Howell's opinion that "the song of the Mocker is easily the most prominent and best loved of southern bird voices—a cheery, rollicking, voluble medley of great variety."

The habit of singing through many days and pouring "cascades of silver down the slope of night," as one poet expressed it, made it a favorite in Arkansas. People found it neighborly and willingly protected "el troubadour."

Tennessee adopted the mocker in a statewide ballot which drew in excess of 70,000 votes. The mockingbird beat out the robin by merely 480 ballots, but easily defeated the Northern Cardinal, Northern Bobwhite, and Eastern Bluebird. Mississippi was the last state to adopt what "might be called our national song-bird" in 1944.

Not everyone supported the mockingbird. The *Dallas Morning News* had nothing against a bird whose "chief contribution to the gayety [*sic*] of the air is in vocal impersonation," but it nominated the indigenous American turkey, "solace for the hardy Texas frontiersman as he was for the early Puritan." This "unruffled explorer of the trackless forest," who has "tickled the palates of uncounted millions" would truly carry the "gospel of Texas to the tables of the effete East," being large in stature and wingspread and as proud in bearing as any peacock (November 15, 1926). The mighty turkey (which was also Ben Franklin's alternative to the Bald Eagle as national symbol) never made it out of the editorial page. More recent press comments suggest that the Golden-cheeked Warbler, the only bird species which nests exclusively in Texas, might be a more appropriate symbol than the widespread mockingbird. Even if this proposal should win support, however, the warbler could lose by default; its numbers are declining while the mocker continues to thrive.

Folklore

*U*nderlying our affection and regard for the mocker is our need to discover deeper messages about our role and place in the universe. We make birds, so visible, colorful, and active around our dwellings, spokesmen for the cosmos and representatives of processes that bind together human lives and make them significant. Ancient literature and many folk traditions treat birds as messengers from the gods. They are signs of nature's organization and rhythms, harbingers of the cycles of planting and harvest.

Mockingbird song, with its power of imitation, captured the attention of aboriginal Americans. Bedichek notes how Biloxi Indians believed that it "mocks one's words"; the Ofo name for it meant "to mock." The Choctaw term *hushi balbaha* referred to the mocker as the bird that speaks a foreign tongue.

The mockingbird is one of about one hundred bird species important in Pueblo Indian ritual, ceremony, and myth. Wise in the ways of song and language, it grants the gift of speech and relates to humans what is happening in other regions. The Pueblo story of creation focuses on emergence from an underworld; animals who preceded or came up into the world with the Pueblos take on special significance. In Hopi myth, for example, first Badger, then Shrike are scouts. Shrike receives promises of land in the upper world, and five days later people emerge. As they do, Mockingbird sits close to the cave entrance from which they come and gives them language. "That is how they got their language, Hopi, American, Navaho, Paiute, Shoshone, and all other Indians," noted religion scholar Elsie Clews Parsons.

Bedichek also relates a legend concerning the "white" mockingbird of Argentina. According to the legend, other bird species resented this mockingbird's powers of song, so that the Great Spirit instructed his messenger to convene a meeting of avians in which he required the white mocker to teach other birds to sing. Grudgingly, the mockingbird sang a fragment to each species, but most of them allowed this sound to degenerate through lack of practice. "Still there are echoes here and there of the great singer's voice in nearly every bird song; and that's the reason . . . people think they hear in the mockingbird's divine and inimitable song certain notes and phrases from other birds. The plagiarism, if any, is the other way around," Bedichek concluded.

A Texas-Mexican folk tale reportedly by Jovita Gonzales accounts for the white on the mockingbird's wings. At one time all animals spoke a common language, Spanish. *El zenzontle,* the mockingbird, was so proud of his song that he grew conceited. "All nature obeys me," he declared to his mate, as blossoms and flowers appeared and humans danced with joy when he sang. Rather than admit the power of God in dressing

MARTIN T. FULFER / TEXAS PARKS & WILDLIFE

up nature in such resplendent colors, the mockingbird exclaimed that "tomorrow I will give a concert to the flowers, and you shall see them sway and dance when they hear me." *"Con el favor de Dios,"* responded his wife, knowing full well that pride blinded her mate.

Next morning as the mockingbird cleared his throat to begin his symphony, a hawk snatched him from the top of a huisache. Terrified, the mockingbird cried, *"Con el favor de Dios,"* admitting that God, not he, decked out the land in its spring glory. Slipping and tumbling into a plowed field he was rescued by a white dove who, as the mocker complained about his torn wings, plucked out his own white feathers to mend them. To this day, the mockingbird bears the dove's white feathers to remind him of overwhelming pride. Those who understand know that he never begins his song without declaring, *"Con el favor de Dios."*

The dull colors of our "many-tongued mimic" are more than compensated for by its powerful, often sustained bursts of song. Charles Hartshorne argues that fine bird songs, like those of the mockingbird, express an individual's entire life for hours, even weeks, at a time. We take notice and admire this expression of continuity, and just as the land's seasons and weather cycles ground our own existence, the songs of birds, its timeless denizens, awaken in us a presence, the belief that there is a connectedness and a sustaining repetition in which we also participate. This minstrel reveals to us its own sense of well-being, so that by listening we can absorb and appreciate a similar fulfilling quality—the thrum of loveliness in the world and of goodness in being alive.

Further Reading

There is a copious literature composed of books, pamphlets, articles in professional and popular journals, novels, poems, and recordings about the mockingbird. This conspicuous bird forced itself on the ken of immigrants over 250 years ago when Mark Catesby included the "Mock-Bird" in celebrating the variety of America's birds in *The Natural History of Carolina, Florida, and the Bahama Islands* (1731; ed. George Frick and Joseph Ewan; Savannah, Ga.: Beehive, 1974). Other bird pioneers, notably Alexander Wilson and John James Audubon, also noted this bird; see Elsa G. Allen, "The History of American Ornithology before Audubon," *Transactions of the American Philosophical Society* 41(1951):386–591. Wilson was especially interested in the "very extraordinary bird," instructing readers in the care of caged individuals (*Wilson's American Ornithology* [1840; reprinted, 1970], pp. 107–115).

Discussion of the relationships of mockingbirds and starlings by Charles G. Sibley and Jon E. Alquist, who summarize taxonomic history, was published in *The Auk* 101(1984):230–243. Careful study of the seasonal activities and breeding behavior of banded mockingbirds originated in Nashville, Tennessee, and Pasadena, California, in the 1930s. Amelia R. Laskey spent more than thirty years researching mockingbirds around her home in Nashville. She banded hundreds, studying territorial behavior and food habits, gaining insight into the species' life history. Harold and Josephine Michener teamed up in the western edge of the bird's range to study mockers in Pasadena. Both sets of authorities published their findings in important ornithological journals. Laskey's several articles appeared in *The Auk*, published by the American Ornithologists' Union (52[1935]:370–381; 61[1944]:211–219; 79[1962]:596–606), *The Wilson Bulletin* (46[1936]:247–255), and *Migrant* (12[1941]:65–67). The Micheners' research appeared in *The Condor* (37[1935]:97–140), a publication of the Cooper Ornithological Club.

Ornithological periodicals are a gold mine of information. In the past decade or so, articles related to food gathering, pairing, territory defense, parental feeding, and fledgling survival have appeared with regularity in *The Auk;* e.g., Roland R. Roth, "Foraging Behavior of Mockingbirds," 96(1979):421– 423; Cheryl A. Logan and Mary Rulli, "Bigamy in a Male Mockingbird," 98(1981):385–386; William T. Joern and James F. Jackson, "Homogeneity of Vegetational Cover around the Nest and Avoidance of Nest Predation in Mockingbirds," 100(1983):497–499; and Randall Breitwisch, Peter G. Merritt, and George H. Whitesides, "Parental Investment by the Northern Mockingbird," 103(1986):152–159. Cheryl A. Logan has investigated the meaning of song for reproduction (*The Auk* 100[1983]:404–413); Randall Breitwisch, Ronald C. Ritter, and Julia Zaias are interested in male bigamy (*The Auk* 103[1986]:424–427); and Keith R. Fulk has noted one instance of polyandry. Fulk's article in *The Wilson Bulletin* (in press) underscores the value of this journal, which has covered wingflashing (George M. Sutton, 58[1946]:206–209; Robert K. Selander and K. D. Hunter, 72[1960]:341–345), range overlap (Beverlea M. Aldridge, 96[1984]:603–618), and song (J. Paul Visscher, 40[1928]:209–217).

The song of the Northern Mockingbird has many devotees. Charles A. Hartshorne, *Born to Sing* (Bloomington: Indiana University Press, 1968), placed the whole family in the very top echelon of the world's songbirds, and Donald J. Borror (*Ohio Journal of Science* 64[1964]:195–207) compares thrush, wren, and mockingbird vocalizations.

Books dealing with state birds usually include sections on the mockingbird's distribution and, in some cases, its arrival and spread. Harry C. Oberholser's two-volume *The Bird Life of Texas* (Austin: University of Texas Press, 1974, vol. 2, pp. 646– 647) notes how widely distributed this species is in Texas; Roy Bedichek's *Adventures with a Texas Naturalist* (rev. ed., Austin: University of Texas Press, 1961, pp. 200–239) gives us the feel for its presence and vitality. Early spread northward in New England and Canada is described by Horace W. Wright (*The Auk* 38[1921]:382–432). Progress into the Midwest and Great Plains is chronicled by Richard R. Graber, Jean W. Graber, and Ethelyn L. Kirk, *Illinois Birds: Mimidae* (Illinois Natural History

Society, *Biological Notes,* No. 68, 1970), pp. 5–13, and Paul A. Johnsgard (*Birds of the Great Plains* [Lincoln: University of Nebraska Press, 1979]), respectively. Up to date details about Mimidae distribution and numbers are recorded in Chandler S. Robbins et al., *The Breeding Bird Survey: Its First Fifteen Years, 1965–1979* (U.S. Fish and Wildlife Service, Resource Publication 157, 1986), pp. 67–71.

The Northern Mockingbird as an "improvement" to avifaunas is summarized by John L. Long, *Introduced Birds of the World* (New York: Universe Books, 1981). John C. Phillips, *Wild Birds Introduced or Transplanted in North America* (U.S. Department of Agriculture, Technical Bulletin No. 61, 1928), documents earlier transplants within the United States.

Lola McGuire Devin, "Birds in American Prose" (M.A. thesis, University of Texas at Austin, 1929), introduces the fascinating picture of birds as important in American letters. A number of nineteenth- and early twentieth-century nature writers recognized this species as singularly American, symbolizing the verve of the new continent. John Burroughs, doyen of turn-of-the-present-century readers committed to nature rambles and outdoor interests, summarized this influence on earlier poets and other writers. In the multivolume work *The Writings of John Burroughs* (Boston: Houghton Mifflin, 1904), vol. 3, *Birds and Poets,* pp. 12–16, and vol. 6, *Fresh Fields,* pp. 138–139, are especially helpful in this regard.

George E. Shankle, *State Names, Flags, Seals, Songs, Birds, Flowers, and Other Symbols* (New York: Wilson, 1934), documents legislative decisions to grant birds official status. Lawmakers selected the mockingbird because it exemplifies qualities that we admire: boldness, tenacity, optimism, etc. Its place in our midst draws us into concerns about sharing the land with native organisms. The list of state birds reminds us of that responsibility to regard wild things not merely as instruments but rather as companions who inspire in us creativity and imagination. They live in our world and we in theirs.

LISTEN TO THE MOCKINGBIRD

Words and Music by Alice Hawthorne

STEVEN HOLT / VIREO

Other Sources

Audubon, John James. *Audubon and His Journals,* ed. Maria R. Audubon, I, 193, 245, 274. New York: Dover, 1960.

———. *The Birds of America,* II, 187–188. New York: Lockwood, 1870.

Bartram, William. *The Travels of William Bartram,* ed. Francis Harper, pp. lx, 7, 39, 196, 218. 1791. Rpt. New Haven: Yale, 1958.

Bent, Arthur Cleveland. *Life Histories of North American Nuthatches, Wrens, Thrashers, and Their Allies,* pp. 295–320. U.S. National Museum Bulletin 195. Washington, D.C.: Smithsonian Institution, 1948.

Berger, Andrew J. *Hawaiian Birdlife,* pp. 194–195. Honolulu: University of Hawaii Press, 1972.

Biedenweg, Douglas W. "Time and Energy Budgets of the Mockingbird (*Mimus Polyglottos*) during the Breeding Season." *The Auk* 100(1983):149–160.

Briggs, Shirley A. "Symbols of States." In *Birds in Our Lives,* ed. Alfred Stafford, pp. 114–120. Washington, D.C., 1966.

British Ornithologists' Union. "Records Committee: Tenth Report," *Ibis* 122(1980):568.

Burleigh, Thomas Dearborn. *Birds of Idaho,* p. 278. Caldwell: Caxton, 1972.

Burnham, George. *Our Canaries and Other Pet Birds,* pp. 106–107. Melrose, Mass., 1878.

Butler, A. G. "Thirty-two Years of Aviculture." *Avicultural Magazine* 5(1914):197.

Coues, Elliott. *Key to North American Birds,* 5th ed., I, 283. Boston: Estes, 1903.

Farrar, C. D. "The Breeding of the American Mockingbird." *Avicultural Magazine* 7(1901):181–184.

———. *Through a Bird-Room Window,* pp. 148–152. London: White, n.d.

Gonzales, Jovita, "Folk Lore of the Texas-Mexican Vaquero." *Publications of the Texas Folk-lore Society,* no. 6(1927):10–11.

Hanson, John. *The American Italy: Southern California,* p. 169. Chicago: Conkey, 1896.

Hartshorne, Charles A. "The Relation of Bird Song to Music. " *Ibis* 100(1958):421–445.

Holden, George H. *Canaries and Cage Birds,* 3d ed., pp. 159, 163. New York, ca. 1895.

Howell, Arthur H. *Florida Bird Life,* p. 356. Tallahassee: Florida Department of Game and Freshwater Fish, 1932.

Hudson, William H. *Birds of La Plata*, I, 11–15. London: Dent, 1920.
———. *The Naturalist in La Plata*, pp. 276–278. London. Dent, 1892.
Jehl, Joseph R., and Kenneth C. Parkes. "Replacements of Landbird Species on Socorro Island, Mexico." *The Auk* 100(1983):551–559.
McAtee, William L. "Useful Birds and Harmful Birds." *Yearbook of the Department of Agriculture (1897)*, p. 670.
Merritt, Peter G. "Group Foraging by Mockingbirds in a Florida Strangler Fig." *The Auk* 97(1980):869–872.
Michelet, Jules. *The Bird*, pp. 277–278. London: Nelson, 1868.
———. In W. H. Davenport Adams and H. Giacomelli, *The Bird World Described with Pen and Pencil*, p. 69. London: Nelson, 1885.
Munro, George C. *Birds of Hawaii*, p. 168. Honolulu: Tongg, 1944.
Nehrling, Henry. *Our Native Birds of Song and Beauty*, I, xlviii–xlix, 51. Milwaukee: Brumder, 1893.
Nuttall, Thomas. In *A Gallery of Birds*, ed. Donald Culress Peatie, pp. 178–179. New York: Dodd Mead, 1939.
Parsons, Elsie Clews. *Pueblo Indian Religion*, I, 239. Chicago: University of Chicago Press, 1939.
Porter, Gene Stratton. *Homing with the Birds*, pp. 113–114. Garden City: Doubleday, Page, 1920.
Robbins, Chandler S. "Prediction of Future Nearctic Landbird Vagrants to Europe." *British Birds* 73(1980):448–457.
Russ, Karl. Quoted by Nehrling, *Our Native Birds of Song and Beauty*, I, 144.
Stewart, Paul A. "Mockingbird Defense of a Winter Food Source." *Journal of Field Ornithology* 51(1980):375.
Stoddard, Herbert L., and Robert A. Norris. "Bird Casualties at a Leon County, Florida, TV Tower: An Eleven-Year Study." *Bulletin of the Tall Timbers Research Station* 8(1967):61.
Sulloway, Frank J. "The *Beagle* Collections of Darwin's Finches (Geospizinae)." *Bulletin of the British Museum (Natural History)*, Zoology Series, 43(1982):49–94, esp. p. 53.
Wilde, Richard Henry. *Richard Henry Wilde: His Life and Selected Poems*, ed. Edward L. Tucker. Athens, Ga.: University of Georgia Press, 1966.